Don't come crying to me when he beats yo' ass!

by

Larry A. Yff

Any of you know someone who plays too much? He always likes to play until somethin' happens and the jokes on him. He will play and play, no matter how many times he's warned, until SMACK!

The person gets tired of warning his ass and smacks him or hits him. Exactly like they said they would. That's the concept behind this book. One more example 1st to make sure we're on the same page...

Another example is the female who likes to hit men. I know a female who always talks shit and has no problem putting her hands on one of her boyfriends, but the minute he smacks her ass or hits her back it's a problem and I would get a phone call. I get a phone call and the conversation always went something like this:

"Hey. Where you at?"

"Why?"

"Well, I need you to come right now. This mutha fucka just gave me a black eye!"

"Why? What did you do?"

"What do you mean, what did I do? I didn't do shit! I can say what I want to his stupid ass!"

"So, you said something to him and he hit you?"

"All I did was tell him he wasn't shit and his mama wasn't shit and he wasn't gonna do shit about it!"

"And then what?"

"Well, there's a little more to it, but it don't matter. You comin?"

"Yes it does matter. And then what?"

"Well, I got in his face and he told me to get out of his face."

"Did you?"

"No."

"Why not? He told you to get out of his face, right?"

"Yeah. But I don't have to do what he says. He ain't my fucking daddy!"

"What happened next?"

"He said, 'I swear to God, if you don't get the fuck out my face, I'm gonna make you get out my face!' and I told him if he's so tough, then make me get out your face.' When I just stood there, he said, 'I promise you. I'm not playing games with you! Get the fuck out my face before you get fucked up!' and I just stood there. I stood there and I was cool until he said 'That's what the fuck I thought!' Once he said that bullshit, I got mad all over again and I smacked him in his face. Then he smacked me in the face so hard I got a black-eye! You gonna help me or not?"

"Bye Felicia."

I know that was a long, drawn-out example, but that's how it usually happens. People need to pay attention when somebody is giving them a warning; especially if they had to repeat themselves.

That was an example similar to the title of the book.

Now, all of my books have something to do with God, Jesus or the Holy Spirit, right? If you're wondering what this has to do with any of them, you don't have to wait any longer because I'm going to tell you: there are certain things Jesus was very serious about that we need to pay attention to.

The things He was extremely serious about, in my view, are the things where He started off His sentence with, "truly" or "verily."

I would have a hard time understanding someone's message if they started it off with that terminology, but it worked for Him and them in that day.

That's why I gave you those 2 examples. You may not understand "truly" or "verily" either, but you understand when someone says, "I promise you" or "I swear to God" or "I put that shit on my dead grandma"

My point is, you know He's serious when He tells you something and He doesn't just tell you. Whenever He adds "truly" or "verily" before a sentence, just look at it like it's His way of saying, "I promise"; except when He says it, you can take that shit to the bank.

If He thinks these things are important, then I do too and that's why I want to go over some of these points He was making.

And in order for the seriousness of His points to make sense, you have to have an understanding and faith in God, Jesus and the Holy Spirit. I'm not using this book to go back and give

you all that history.

If you know the truth about the information the Bible

shares with us about God, then this message is for you.

If you don't know the truth about the information the

Bible shares with us about God, this message is also for you. It

will let you in on His personality, mentality and what you need to

pay attention to once you come over to His side of things.

We won't go over all of them. We'll go over the ones I

think are tied into some sort of lesson for us. Let's go...

Do you know the song where Jay-Z said, "I got 99 problems

and a bitch ain't one?" Well, it's little smart-ass, cocky-ass

comments like this that have made me shy away from him, even

though he is very talented, rich as fuck and gets to sleep with

Beyonce every night. Here's why...

Even though he says his name is "Jay-Z", he also likes to call himself "Hova" or "Jay-Hova" as in Jehovah as in Jesus. I guess you may say that's not a comparison to being holy like Jesus, but I gotta disagree and it's the "I got 99 problems and a bitch ain't one" part that is my reasoning.

"And if he finds it, truly I tell you, he is happier about that one sheep than about the 99 that did not wander off." Sound familiar? No. No it's not Jay-Z aka Jay-Hove. That "truly" comes from the Jesus aka Jehovah and even though He talked in parables, I can pretty much guarantee He was not referring to the 99 sheep as being problems or as the 1 being a bitch.

In the parable about the Lost Sheep, he was giving them a situation about a man who owned 100 sheep. In this story, he had 100 sheep and if one had wandered off, the shepherd would leave the 99 and look for the lost one.

He said He was using that parable to refer to God's mentality about us. He loves it when we are faithful, like the 99, but at the same time, if one of gets off track and He is able to reach that one and bring Him back, He is just as happy with that one as He was with the faithful 99.

In fact, He doesn't view any of us that get lost as being a problem. We are still His and Jesus was saying God will do whatever it takes, and He likes to do this, to make sure none of us winds up not enjoying life the way He designed it. Getting back to Jay-Z...

Do you think it was a coincidence he just so happens to refer to himself as "Jay-Hova" and references a parable from Jesus who is commonly referred to as Jehovah? Take it how you want. I'm just laying some shit out there for you to look at. Moving on...

"Truly I tell you, whatever you bind on Earth will be bound in Heaven and whatever you loose on Earth will be loosed in Heaven..."

I started with this one because this is my most favoritest one! This is the one that made me look at Jesus in more of a political light than a religious or a church perspective and it was also the "truly I tell you" that got me excited the most!

What He was guaranteeing me I could do things on Earth that would legally be binding in Heaven....

Hmmmm...

Think about that for a serious minute...

"Whatever you bind on Earth is legally binding in Heaven". Now why in the fuck do you think I'm so excited about this "truly"??? Well, I'm glad you asked, Reader. Here's why:

When you know the law, you become confident. If you don't know the law, you are at a disadvantage. Quick example:

If you get pulled over by the police and know the law or are white, you are confident. I'm just kidding about the white part, but I had to throw that in to see if you were paying attention.

Well, I'm kinda kidding and kinda not. The law in America said, "only people with white skin and European heritage can become citizens". There were other laws related to skin color that allowed white people to lynch, kill, rape, discriminate, treat unfairly anybody without white skin and legally get away with it.

This mentality transferred to the police. Police across the country were routinely used to fuck black people up and that mentality still lingers since the inception of American police forces.

If you're black and get pulled over, a police officer is a lot quicker to shoot you or talk to you in a degrading manner like he's superior to you somehow.

If you're white and get pulled over, knowing the history of police from a different lens allows you to chat with them unafraid and un-irritated like you guys are old buddies.

I mention this because your view and experience with the law is a very important matter. Jesus said He came to fulfill the Law. He is all about establishing God's Law in all the world's systems and He is telling us "whatever we do on Earth can be legally binding in Heaven."

Later on we will be talking about the Lord's Prayer. In this prayer we are supposed to do daily, Jesus said we are supposed to include a statement in that prayer/petition that goes something like this: may your kingdom come and may your will be done on Earth like it is in Heaven.

Well, Reader, once I started to connect the dots between

and realized God is the Being who created everything and Jesus

actually is the one, true, biological-in-nature Son of God, I knew

that particular prayer held weight. It held power. It held hidden

earthly and spiritual power...and I wanted some!

As I began to realize God's purpose for humanity, based on

what Jesus said, is to establish Heaven on Earth, I found my true

calling and purpose. I was designed by God to be used by Him to

establish Heaven on Earth!

Remember, God can't legally just come to Earth and

correct everything. That would be illegal because He legally gave

control of the world's systems and Earth's resources to humans

and therefore, He has to wait for a human to ask or petition God

to intervene!

If yo' ass ain't jumpin' out of your seat right now realizing

how much power and purpose you have, your ass must not be

able to read English well and it would benefit you to get an interpreter pretty fuckin' fast. Either that or wait until a copy of this book comes out in a language where you know exactly what the fuck is being said. Don't miss this shit right here, Reader!

So, God needs humans to legally establish His power and authority on Earth. If I pray the Lord's Prayer, I am now legally opening myself up to be one of those humans God can work through, right?

Do you see where I'm going with this? If so, congratulations…keep reading! If not, don't worry about it…keep reading!

God can now begin to download plans to take over the world's education system if that's something on your heart and he'll use the Holy Spirit to be your guide. The Holy Spirit knows the future, so whatever He tells you to do will be succeed even if you don't see it working right away.

God now can begin to download plans to you to take over the environment at your place of work. It doesn't matter if you work for some billion-dollar company and are an executive or a part of the maintenance team: you have the same opportunity to become an influencer for God at that company.

I don't think you're getting what I'm saying, so I'm gonna take it one step further for you and I hope the words start screaming and jumping off the fucking pages and slap you right in the middle of your forehead!!!

IF YOU ASK GOD TO USE YOU TO GET HIS NAME, RESPECT AND GLORY OUT INTO THE WORLD, HE CAN LEGALLY GIVE YOU ACCESS TO ANY EARTHLY RESOURCES LIKE OIL, MONEY, A CLASSROOM, A CAR OR WHATEVER ELSE THE FUCK YOU NEED SO YOU CAN COMPLETE YOUR GOD-GIVEN AGENDA!

Don't forget: the Earth is God's. He created it. He designed it and He owns it. We are simply managers of it. He did not give it to us. What He did give us was control and we fucked that up through Adam, but Jesus legally came and straightened it all out and gave us humans control back.

We do not own the Earth. We don't own shit! Whatever we use or have is to be used on this Earth. Nobody takes shit with them from this life to the next, no matter how hard you try.

That reminds of something off topic really quick: back in the day, Egyptians put gold and other valuable things in the caskets of the Pharoah's so they could use it in the afterlife. Do you know how we know this? Funny thing is, they died and weren't able to take shit with them! It was all left in the caskets, duh. How else do you think we know about all the gold and shit?

Getting back on track...

We are the legal managers of this place we call Earth and if you become one of the ones who wants to manage the Earth's resources and do it according to the owner's way…your ass shouldn't be able to fail!

In the event you do fail, it won't be because you didn't have all the financial or natural resources you needed. You must have fucked up along the way somewhere and God had to bench you for a little bit.

Imagine that! Do you know how confident and cocky you would be if you personally knew the owner of Amazon? If you knew Jeffrey, you would have access to a whole lot of products and power; but if you knew the owner of the entire Earth, you can have access to a whole lot more products and power!

You'd have access to all the world's resources! Every drop of oil or water! Every piece of gold, diamond and copper!

Alright, I've gotta come down from that and talk about some other "trulys". I hate to leave this one, but we gotta go, Reader…

"Truly I tell you, until Heaven and Earth disappear, not the smallest letter, not the least stroke of a pen, will by any means disappear from the Law until everything is accomplished."

Right before He made that sentence He said, "Don't think I came to abolish the Law or the Prophets..." He made a point to say the Law will be accomplished, but what does that mean? Several things of significance, but let's focus on anything law-related.

He was giving His 1st sermon and He was letting the people know even though He was here talking about some things that sound contradictory to the Law and the Prophets, that wasn't His objective.

At the time of His 1st lesson, the Law required sacrifices for sin and the Prophets were all prophesying about the coming Messiah. The King of the Jews.

What the crowd didn't know was years later, Jesus' death legally would legally qualify as the human blood sacrifice the Laws of sacrifice required and He also fulfilled what the Prophets were talking about because He had arrived.

Jesus is the Messiah.

If you want to go deeper and get more technical into qualifications and sacrifices, you have to get a different book by a different author. I don't have the Bible degrees a professional Bible person has and they like getting involved in long-ass, heated discussions. I don't.

So like I was saying, Jesus fulfilled the Law and what the Prophets were talking about and that is something to dig into deeper, at your convenience, because He started off talking about the Law and the Prophets with, "...truly I tell you..."

"Truly I tell you, if you give to the needy and make a big deal about it so others can see how good and philanthropic you are, you have received the reward you are looking for…"

Jesus was talking about the need to help those in need and He was telling people how they should do it. He was telling them anyone who helps people in need will get a reward.

He would go on to say these same people had the opportunity to choose what their reward would be. You could be loud about it and have your reward being the general public or you could do an act of kindness *in the dark* and get a reward from God.

What reward do you want? Jesus was guaranteeing us that there is definitely a reward for helping, so choose wisely, Reader.

"Truly I tell you, when you pray, don't be loud about that either. I mean, you can, but like I told you when we were talking

about fasting: there is a reward for praying and you get to choose what your reward will be."

Jesus said pretty much the same thing He said about getting a reward for proper prayer as He did for helping people in need, but He took it a step further and helped us.

He helped us because He told us the proper way to pray in order to get a reward from God. Remember, Reader, we can get a reward from people around us or from God. I know this is true because Jesus kept saying "truly" in front of a lot of things that dealt with rewards.

What the reward from God will be He did not say, but from what I know about God's reward system, that shit has got to be better than simply having a bunch of people look at you like you're such a benevolent, giving, loving person.

This is where He gave us what we call the Lord's Prayer. When you pray this prayer on a daily basis, you are guaranteed to be rewarded by God somehow on a daily basis.

During my addictions, I needed to see daylight. I needed some type of reward. I needed something to keep me motivated to stay in the fight and continue to work through my addictions and the Lord's Prayer for me was an excellent place to start.

I began to say this prayer every day. If I woke up sober, I said the Lord's Prayer. If I hadn't been to sleep yet because I was high as fuck, instead of jacking off to help me cum down from my cocaine high, I began to say the Lord's Prayer.

Yupper, I said it and talked to God smack dab in the middle of my addiction and it gave me strength to keep going. It was symbolic for me to know, since Jesus guaranteed it, that I would still be able to get some type of reward from God...even while I wasn't fully recovered yet.

"Truly I tell you, if anyone gives even a cup of cold water to one of these people I am sending out as one of my disciples, that person certainly will certainly not lose their reward."

Jesus had just sent out a group of about 72 people to go out and teach people what He had been teaching them. He values them so much that He was pretty much giving anyone who helped them a guaranteed reward.

These 72 students of Jesus were supposed to go from village to village and share the message Jesus focused on which was telling people how to become citizens of the Kingdom of Heaven.

He told them to go out there and don't take any money or nothin'. He instructed them to stay at the house of people who welcomed them, but in the event a city didn't want them there, they were to keep it movin'.

On the flipside, if somebody helped one of His disciples in the very smallest of ways, giving them one cup of cold water, they were guaranteed to get some type of reward that no matter what that person did for the rest of his life, his reward couldn't be taken from him.

That's a powerful ass statement and a powerful ass reward!

"Truly I tell you that if any two of you on earth agree about anything they ask for, it will be done for them by my Father in Heaven. For where 2 or 3 gather in my name, I'll be with them."

You have to remember all these "trulys" are things that have power. They are backed by the creator of the universe and His Son. These "trulys" have power whether Republicans or Democrats are in power. These "trulys" come with lifetime guarantees and by lifetime, I'm talking here on Earth and the

afterlife.

I mentioned that because a lot of them are extremely

simple for being so fucking powerful! Jesus is saying if there is a

problem on earth that goes against God's laws and you want to fix

it, you literally have to find someone who also believes in God,

have a sit-down and agree 1) there's a problem and 2) you have

the faith Jesus is the Son of God and as such, Him and God now

have the legal right to intervene on humanity's sake and get shit

cleared up! Let me go personal with you…

My wife and I are on the same track when it comes to all

things God and Jesus. So when we are watching tv and we see

commercials by "legal" drug companies who are pushing all these

drugs that 1) don't actually cure shit and 2) have a shit-ton of

negative, addicting side effects or will kill you…we get mad!

We're both on the same page that these large drug

companies don't give a shit about the health and well-being of

people who feel like they have to take drugs for healing and since

the drugs are destroying our bodies and our bodies somehow

house the Holy Spirit…we gotta shut these big companies down.

You see how simple that is? We both agree 1) there is a

problem and 2) somebody is intentionally doing something that

goes against the good of humanity and 3) they are typically

getting their products cleared by paying off congressmen and

government agencies that should be looking out for their

constituents.

Since we believe in the power of this "truly", we look at

each other, discuss the problem and say, "Okay, why don't you

put that request in with the team."

That's all we have to do. These are things we want to fight against anyways, so it goes without saying that we include "...and use us to help lead the fight, please."

And it is finished.

My advice to you is find a partner and start searching. Start searching and googling shit on the computer and when you find things that need to be fixed that are blatantly out there going against God's Laws, simply put in the request knowing Jesus is somehow in the midst and between Him, God and the Holy Spirit...shit will get straightened out ASAP!

That's part of the beauty of "trulys"...you aren't limited to a certain industry or location. Jesus said you can use this "truly" for any situation that is designed to correct something and bring it back under the control of God.

If you're gonna use this one, go big please! Don't fuck around and waste it on trying to correct the way one person is doing something wrong.

I mean, don't get me wrong, any "truly" in this category holds weight like a mutha fucka and you have the right to use it how you want, I'm just saying with all the stuff about trying to teach little kids that being a transexual is cool and a bunch of other crazy shit...let's go big, baby!!

"Truly I tell you it will be more bearable for Sodom and Gomorrah on the day of judgement than for that town."

A couple of "truly's" ago, there was one that had to do with Jesus sending about 70 of His students out to teach people about the Kingdom of Heaven. Part of His instructions was to go to a city and if they don't want to hear what they're saying, don't sweat it.

Jesus told them to not stress it, keep going to another city and basically say "fuck 'em". This is the backdrop to this truly.

There was a city we read about in the earlier manuscripts found in the Bible about Sodom and Gomorrah. These cities were known for having a lot of corruption including, but not limited to, homosexual activity.

I'm only singling homosexual activity out because it's relevant to the story, but trust me, there was a whole lot of other sinful shit goin' on in those 2 towns! Anyways...

A man named Lot lived on the outskirts of those towns and he was Abraham's nephew. You know, the Abraham who had the hot-ass wife and was tested by God to sacrifice his son Isaac?

Well, God was going to destroy both of these towns and decided He would spare Lot and his family because of Lot's faith in Him. So God sent 2 angels to give Lot a head's up. God gave Lot a break only because he was Abraham's nephew.

The Bible says, "…when the men and young boys of the city of Sodom saw the 2 men who were Lot's guests, they surrounded Lot's house and told Lot to bring his guests out so they could have sex with them. Lot said "no" and right before they rushed Lot and his house to get at the 2 "men", the angels pulled Lot back in the house and made all the men and boys that had came to have sex with them go blind…"

Lot was able to escape and once he left the vicinity of Sodom, God started the show! He made fire and some other lava-type shit rain down on both cities and destroyed them completely.

In the "truly" we're talking about, Jesus said the residents of Sodom and Gomorrah will have it better off than any town who doesn't want to hear what any of His chosen 70 disciples have to say!

Sodom and Gomorrah got off light? Do you know how horrible of a death that would be to have it rain and the raindrops are a combination of acid, hot lava and fire? That shit would be miserable!

But remember, Reader, Jesus said "truly" before He talked about the fate of any city who didn't listen to the 72. That means, He was sending them out and letting them know not only did He have their back, they had God as their back and to boost their confidence, He gave them the example of Sodom and Gomorrah as a guarantee of what would happen, so they could stay focused on the task at hand.

For me, that would definitely have been a good pep talk. I'm about to go out into the world and do a lot of the business plans God has for me and if Jesus said, "Hey Larry. Just so you know...when you approach a media company I send you to that is corrupt and you want to buy them and they refuse, don't even worry about it.

Just keep heading out to the other companies. Remember God's track record of destroying entire cities and masses of wealth for people who didn't fall in line? Well, I will make that company have so many failures that they will be begging you to come back and buy them!

And when you sit down at the table the 2nd time, the terms will be so favorable for you! You'll be able to buy them for pennies on the dollar!"

"Truly I tell you, if you have faith as small as a mustard see, you can say to this mountain, 'Move from here to there' and it will move. Nothing will be impossible for you."

This is another one of them powerful ass "trulys" that you need to pay attention to! He said you will literally have the ability to make a literal mountain literally move from one place to another!

Do you know how fucking impossible that is to picture? It seems impossible, but if he put "truly" in front of that statement, you can guarantee it can be done!

What I like about that statement is He went big. Jesus went big to get His point across. He didn't say you would be able to make a tree fall down or weeds stop growing in your front yard just by saying "stop". He said you can move a mountain!

It does seem crazy at 1st, but I'll be it didn't seem too crazy when He did pretty much what He told them they could do when He did what He did with nature. What He did isn't the stuff fairy tales are made of. They were documented events in history by several, credible sources.

Nobody has ever stopped a storm…He did.

Nobody has ever walked on water…He did.

This was a situation that arose because someone had approached Jesus and asked Him to get rid of a demon from his son or somebody in his family. His disciples told Jesus this was a tough demon and none of them could get rid of it.

Jesus told them if they only had a little bit of faith, maybe about as big as a mustard seed, they could literally move mountains and then He walked up to the possessed man and told the demon to leave and it did.

Jesus is telling us what a little bit of faith can do. Does that excite you? Having just a little bit of faith has a ton of power and I know it's true not only because Jesus said it, but because of the media.

I hate most movies. The ones that seem to be the most popular make humans look like we're just a bunch of weak pussy's and punks.

We always have to try and band together to fight some more intelligent and powerful life form that comes from some other galaxy. Somebody from "out there" always wants to come to Earth and harvest humans and all our natural resources and the only way we can do it is, according to the movies, is have just a little bit of faith...in humanity.

You see, I believe Satan has been taking full advantage of the legal right he once had over the world's systems and knowing how influential the media is, that became one of his babies.

He takes themes and truths from the Bible and the Lost Books of the Bible and has been slipping them into thousands of mainstream movies and twisting the biblical process.

Take faith for instance. There are hundreds of movies over the years that push the concept of the power of faith, but they do it in a twisted way.

The focus of faith has been twisted away from having faith in God to having faith in anything but God. Satan has been able to influence movie producers to put out movies that teach us about the power of faith, but instead of putting that real power to use in the proper, spiritual way with God, we are constantly being told to believe in Santa Claus for presents or in Jack Frost.

I have literally stopped going to movies and I am going to literally start buying media companies and shutting down all their attempts to make faith seem like yes, it is a real thing and yes, it has actual power, but no, don't tap into the power of faith...tap into the mystical power of faith by believing in Santa.

I saw a Christmas movie one time with Will Ferrell. "Elf". That's the name of the movie. In this movie, Santa Clause couldn't power up his sleigh.

He said he needed the power of faith from little boys and girls to power it. When it crashed, a little boy told a bunch of onlookers that "you all need to help Santa! He needs us! He needs us to believe in him!"

After he said that, he got everybody to say, "Yes, I believe in you Santa" and sure enough, Santa's power boosters got stronger and stronger as the people cheered and shouted that they had faith in Santa.

Their faith in Santa powered up the boosters and "Christmas" was saved. I put it in aprentheseis because Santa doesn't have shit to do with the real meaning of Christmas.

Oh! I'm gonna insert a quick Private Matter Bonus Essay I wrote about Santa. Check it out:

YOU CAN'T KILL SANTA CLAUS

You can't kill Santa because he is fake. He is a cartoon hero. He never took an actual breath of air. Why am I dissing Santa? Santa gets the middle finger because society is trying to push make-believe characters like him as being real as a distraction from the real meaning of Christmas and it's time somebody stood up and said, "Fuck Santa".

People find it somewhat easy to believe in God as well as ghosts, angels and demons, but somehow don't believe in Satan.

In my view, Satan is behind the whole make-believe and magical world of Santa so that we take the focus from Jesus and His life to Santa.

I'm going to go so far to say Satan is so obvious with it, that if you take the name "Santa" and spin a few letters around you will get "Satan". What if...

Since we're talking about movies and certain ways I believe Satan is influencing it, I might as well slide this other Private Matter Bonus Essay in about his sneaky ass too. Check this one out and then we'll get back in to some more "trulys":

SATAN and DEMONS in MOVIES

One thing that I began to wonder about when I was looking for images of God, Jesus and angels in the media was their image. Whoever is their publicity manager sucks!

The egotistical nature of Satan is apparent by the way he influences main street media. Every time there is a demon, he is usually as big as a skyscraper, breathes fire, can destroy anything and everyone, has gigantic muscles and usually his mouth is full of sharp-ass, metal-cutting teeth! The demons are seen as being unstoppable and menacing.

What images do you see of angels? They are typically old women clucking around the stove baking cookies. If there is an angel in the movie that is portrayed as a man, he isn't the most masculine fella. He gets the hero role because he has a good heart and fights for the good of humanity; meanwhile, the bad guy is some muscle-bound, cigarette smoking, bad-ass biker dude dressed in all black. What the fuck?

As a believer, I know Jesus, God, angels and Satan are all real. I also know from history that God kicked Satan out of Heaven. I also know Jesus tells us that He ain't worried about Satan at all and that Satan has no hold on Him. Then there are the recorded wars we hear about where the angels in Heaven demolished the fallen angels, aka demons.

With all those historical facts and data, why would the media get the ideal that Satan and his band of merry men are super powerful and that God and His warrior angels are mild-mannered, middle-aged white men who wear dress shoes, khaki pants and blazers?

When you look at people who say they worship the Devil or musicians who play what they call "Devil music", do they look happy to you? Most of the time, they try and look as dark, powerful, rude, wild and "evil" as possible. They are trying to represent the powerful, dark spirits of the devil they see in the

media. If they knew the truth and that they are really walking around representing the losing team...

Anywho, as soon as my wife and I get our money up, we will be on the frontline with our media companies showing real images of the real spiritual powers that be.

I was excited when I came across a media company that claimed to have all Christian movies. I skimmed through the movies and they all looked soft. They all had the same images of angels and God that the Satan-influenced media portrayals had! I saw one movie where God was portrayed as a woman! Whatever!!!!

Alright, let's get back in to the book...

Before we leave the "truly" we're on, did you see the very last part of it? Just in case you didn't, I'll tell you what it said. It said "Nothing will be impossible for you."

How's that for some more power!?! You see, people who don't believe in God, and a lot of people who do, feel like they are powerless to the world.

I was watching a video called "The Levels of Wealth" and it was saying all the benefits of wealth and the differences between them. The focus was on material things and influence.

At the millionaire stage, you don't really have a lot of influence, but you can definitely live a comfortable life.

At the stage of having anywhere from $1M to $50M, the guy said you are now able to have influence in your circles and society and you can buy whatever you want.

When you get above that level and stop just shy of the $1Billion-dollar level, there is nothing you can't have and nothing you can't do. You can buy whatever you want and have people do whatever you want.

And then there's the level of multi-billion-dollar status. Here's the level where the guy said you can influence not only friends and family or a company or two, now you can influence entire industries and country political systems.

It's true. I hate to say it, but that is true regarding wealth. But here's the thing, nobody's on the billion-dollar level is using wealth to influence society for God.

Jeff Bezos of Amazon has a lot of wealth. He doesn't believe in God and he wants to move humanity to the Moon.

Elon Musk of Tesla has a lot of wealth. He doesn't believe in God and he wants to move humanity to Mars.

The rest of the people on the top of the list don't mention God and are only interested in using their influence on countries and politics for their own personal or business gain.

Why am I talking about influence when the "truly" we are on is talking about faith? I'm talking about it because if you want to influence the media, the government, our education systems or any other area of society, once again, all it takes is a drop of faith.

Jesus said a drop of faith in Him and NOTHING IS IMPOSSIBLE. Nothing is impossible. I have to say it one more time so it sinks into your brains that all it takes is a very small belief in Jesus and His divinity and NOTHING will be impossible for you and that means EVERYTHING will be possible for you!

"Truly I tell you, wherever this gospel is preached throughout the world, what she has done will also be told, in memory of her."

This "truly" is pretty cool. I like it because, well, because it's more proof that every, single time Jesus said "truly" and then some other stuff...it either happened or will happen. In this example, it's something we might overlook as small and insignificant, but it hammers home the need to listen to Jesus when He says "truly".

There was a woman who approached Jesus and as she did, she opened a jar of expensive perfume and poured some slowly on his head...Jesus did not complain, but His disciples watching did.

They started to get mad at her, explaining that was a waste of expensive perfume. Expensive perfume that could have been sold and the proceeds from the sale used to help the needy.

Jesus told them to calm down and explained what she did was a beautiful thing and because of this one act, history will not forget her.

Isn't that significant? Here we have a lady whose name we don't know who is only mentioned one time in the entire manuscripts and documents that make up the Bible...and her cameo is included!

Let me put it to you this way, the Bible is made up of 66 manuscripts we call books. They were selected from thousands of historically accurate manuscript, letters and sacred scriptures.

There were several committees of people who were involved in this process and, well, it was a tough-ass job. Their job was to sift through all of these documents and narrow it down as best as possible to get the entire message of God from creation until Jesus returning to Heaven…all in a travel-size book.

Everything of significance to them was added. A lot of scriptures were taken out for a variety of reasons. From what I heard about this process, the criteria to get in the 66 books was extremely hard.

In fact, it is a known fact there may be bits and pieces missing or changed from the 66 books that made the cut.

With all this juggling, cutting, removing and rewriting of thousands of scriptures…they felt the need to include this one little story?

At the time, I'm sure they weren't like, "Well, we have to include this little part to make sure what Jesus said came true." I know this because even the author of the book we call Luke, I think it was, acknowledged there was no way to make a manuscript that documented all of the miracles and teachings of Jesus.

But somehow, this little, two-paragraph event made it into the Bible and we all are still reading about it thousands of years later…just like Jesus said thousands of years earlier!

"Truly I tell you, one of you will betray me." Jesus was eating what we call the Last Supper when He said this "truly".

He knew it would be His last meal before somebody, somebody currently in the room, would betray Him. He was eating this meal with His close 12 disciples, so for Him to make that statement, even though He said "truly" in front of it, seemed like this "truly" may not be true.

Why would it be true? Everyone at the table was a loyal disciple of His. Could it be possible this is the one "truly" that didn't come true?

No. This one shockingly came true just like He said.

They were eating and after Jesus said this, one by one they started asking Jesus was it them. Let's stop there for a minute...

Jesus said one of them was going to betray Him and they're all asking *Him* which one of them will it be. Did you catch that? They trust everything Jesus says so much that, even though none of the disciples had any plans to betray Him, they weren't sure somehow.

It was as though they didn't trust themselves. "It's not me, is it?" Why in the fuck would you even have to ask that? Is it you? Have you been making plans to have Him killed? I see why

Jesus was always asking them, "Are you seriously that dumb?"

So, He didn't directly answer them; instead He said, "All

I'm saying is the person who's gonna betray me is definitely in this

room. He's gonna be in so much trouble that it would be better

off if he was never born than to be the one who betrays me."

Immediately after He made that comment, Judas, the one

who had already made plans to have Jesus arrested that night,

said to Jesus, "You're not talking about me, are you?"

Jesus is so cool! He is so mutha fuckin' cool! Guess what

He said? He said, "I didn't say it...you did." Jesus was already

over it. He knew it and He knew Judas knew it, so it wasn't any

sense in playing games at this point of the night.

After the meal, Jesus would go off and pray by Himself like

He liked to do. When He was finished praying, Judas approached

Him with a group of religious leaders and armed guards.

Judas said, "Hey, Jesus" but Jesus didn't say "hi" back. Once again, Jesus was cool with His destiny and knew part of it included being the blood sacrifice that would pay the price for sin and legally give humans control of the world's systems again, so all He said was, "Do what you gotta do, Bro."

And they did. They arrest Him and this leads to that and He gets hung on a cross and dies. His death played out exactly how He said and by now, Reader, you should have known it would have ended that way.

Why should you have known? Because Jesus started His death-prediction with the words "truly".

What you may not know is the fate of Judas. Once Jesus is in custody, Judas gets paid. He was okay with it until he saw the religious leaders sealing the fate of Jesus by having him appear before the Governor from Rome who ruled that area.

They took Him there and requested that He be executed. Hearing these words, we learn Judas gave the religious leaders their money back and killed himself out of shame and guilt.

"Truly I tell you, this very night, before the rooster crows, you will disown me 3 times." This "truly" was another one He gave during the Last Supper. It was as though Jesus was like, "Well, this is it so before I go, I'm gonna let all you know what's gonna happen and who's gonna do what and when before I go…"

He said this "truly" to Peter. Peter was known as the disciple who was always ready to stand up for Jesus. There was an event in history where Jesus was walking on water during a storm and approached the boat Peter and some other disciples were in.

Peter was the bold one and asked Jesus if he could come out there and meet Him. Jesus said it was cool, so, Peter the bold, stepped over the boat and began to walk on water for a couple of seconds.

I think there was a lot of talk in the room and a lot of unspoken shit when Jesus told the disciples the person who was gonna betray Him was in the room. I personally think He gave Peter this "truly" to let Peter know that at any point and time, we all can do some things that we think we would never do.

I think Peter was confident in knowing he wasn't the one who was going to betray Jesus.

I think Peter was cocky in his walk with Jesus and I think Jesus was letting him know that even the most righteous, devoted follower of His could stumble sometimes...just like Judas.

I have to take you on a quick bunny trail and hop to a different topic and talk about a man named Job...

There was a man named Job who was tested by Satan.

God personally let Satan do whatever he wanted, except kill him,

as a way of testing Job's faith in God.

Satan used his powers and abilities to kill all of Job's kids,

have all of his wealth stolen and make Job have some type of

nasty, itchy, painful skin condition that included bumps full of

puss all over his body. Job didn't waver. He never cussed God

out.

He was close. He was close as fuck. He was probably as

close as any human being could be to cussing God out and having

a "Goddamn!" moment...but he didn't. And for that, his story was

included in the history book we call the Bible for everyone to

learn from.

I went on this side trail because there was more to the

picture of Job's life that I hadn't noticed until about my 50th time

reading his story and it relates to Peter. Here me out...

While Job was going through his testing period, at one point he said, "...I don't like this! I used to be the man. Everyone listened to me when I spoke. Everybody bowed down to me. I was treated like royalty and I had a lot of wealth...but now, now **my worst fear has come true...**"

Do you see the connection to Peter? Here, let me help you out a little...

Peter was thinking he was such a good, devoted student of Jesus that there was absolutely no way he would betray Him. He was confident in his ability, but Jesus had to let Peter know no matter how confident you are, shit can still happen. Enter Job...

He was enjoying life and all his wealth and respect people were giving him. He had it good. He had a wife, wealth and respect, but there was something hidden in him that he needed to face.

When Satan approached God and asked God's permission to tempt Job, God said "yes". I believe God allowed this temptation so Job could deal with an issue he wanted to cover up.

You see, even though he was known for having faith in God, he still had fear in his heart. He still had a fear of, "What if I lose all my shit? Will I still love God? Will I still be happy? What would I do without all the money, power and respect I have?"

God is so wise!!! Here Satan was thinking God was allowing him to wreak havoc in the life of one of God's faithful's when in reality God was using Satan to help one of His faithful's realize there was a hole in his faith that needed to be dealt with!

Job found his answer: even if I lose my shit, I have enough faith to understand God has a plan for everything.

Now, don't get it twisted. Job was cussing everybody and everything out! He told his friends he hated the day he was born and wished his mama never had him and he even went so far as to say he wished his mama was never born just to make sure she never had him, but he never cussed God out. Getting back on track with Peter...

When Jesus told Peter the "truly" about him denying Jesus 3 times before the rooster crowed, Peter flat out said that could never happen. Do you see his defiance, Reader?

Jesus started the sentence off with "truly" and Peter was too bold to acknowledge it. Shit. I have to get off track super quick again...

I find myself in the same shoes as Peter sometimes. I say this because I know Jesus is telling the truth and what He says is the absolute truth, but there are some things I think don't apply to me.

When Jesus gave the parable about the 10 or 12 virgins, I was like, "The ones who didn't keep oil in their lamps so they would have enough light to be ready when the man they were looking for appeared, they deserve to be left out in the cold dark

of night with no light!"

This parable was about a bunch of young girls who decided

to wait for the groom of a recent wedding to come by the place

they were at. This is back in the day, so they had lamps that were

fueled by oil. Maybe kerosene.

As it got dark, they all fell asleep when suddenly somebody

said, "He's coming! He's coming!"

They all woke up when they heard this and headed out to

meet the groom, but apparently half of them didn't bring any

extra kerosene. They weren't prepared to cover all their bases in

the event the groom came so late that they would be low on fuel.

The women who were prepared and had extra kerosene

poured their reserve oil in their lamps and went out to meet the

groom; while the unprepared ones ran back home to get more

kerosene, but by then they had missed the groom.

The lesson in this parable was Jesus is the groom. He refers to Himself as being the groom and the church He was establishing, not the churches we have today but I'm not gonna go there right now, is the bride.

He loved the church and He was saying He was committed to it like a husband is committed to his wife in marriage.

He often talked about leaving and them coming back. This parable hinted at the fact that He indeed had to leave, but when He comes back, and nobody but God knows when that day is scheduled to happen, whoever is in His church better be ready.

He was saying we need to live every day like He may be coming. We're supposed to be prepared for Him to come any day. We're supposed to be prepared like the young girls who had extra kerosene.

I was feeling cocky prior to this parable. I was feeling good with my spiritual walk and just knew I would always be on point and ready if Jesus was to pop up. I was feeling like the young

virgins who brought the extra kerosene for their lamps.

I just knew I was doing good and controlling my addictions

to cocaine and porn and Jesus could come whenever He

wanted...He wouldn't catch me off-guard smokin' crack and

watchin' porn in somebody's basement!

And then it happened! I had been drug-free for one of the

longest periods in my life and then BAM! I had a couple of

triggers hit me in the same day and I got high all night. The very

thing I was saying could never happen to me, that could never

happen to on-the-right-path Larry, happened!

That was humbling for me and I will never forget it. I will

never forget it and I told myself I would do my best to remember

that incident in the event a pastor or somebody who is on a solid

path in life happens to get off track.

I have to remember even me, during a time when I was in a zone with having custom t-shirt graphic designs made up for my clothing line and writing a book a week…even during that "righteous" season, I too messed up.

Okay, let's get back to Peter. I stopped 2 times already and if I stop again, I won't find my way back and that means you will be lost as well. Let's go…

So Peter says to Jesus there's now way this "truly" is going to come true. Absolutely no way. He went so far as to tell Jesus he was willing to give his life before he did something that could be viewed as betrayal.

If I could have gone back in time I would have said, "Yo, Peter. Don't do it! Don't think it can't be you! You know what happens when Jesus says 'truly' before something. Whatever follows that word is going to come true no matter how much you think it won't!"

But I wasn't there to tell him and none of the other

disciples told him either, but it became very obvious, starting after

the Last Supper, that Peter was going to fuck up, just like Jesus

said. Let's do a play by play:

1. Jesus tells Peter he will deny knowing Him

2. Peter tells Jesus He's wrong

3. Jesus takes Peter and 2 other disciples to go with Him and

    just keep Him company while He prays

4. Peter and the other 2 fall asleep and Jesus is irritated

    with them

5. Jesus tells them to stay awake and that He was going to

    pray again in private

6. Peter and the other 2 fall asleep for the second time and

    Jesus is irritated

7. Jesus goes off to pray again and tells them to stay awake

8. Peter and the other 2 fell asleep for the 3rd time

Did you see what was happening? Here was Peter the Bold telling Jesus He would never leave or betray Jesus and here he was, within an hour of Jesus saying the Peter-related "truly", Peter fell asleep and basically left Jesus hanging 3 times!

Jesus had said before the rooster crowed 3 times Peter would deny knowing Jesus and the rooster was still asleep! It was still nighttime and Peter was fuckin' up already! There's more…

After the 3rd time Peter and the 2 disciples fell asleep, Jesus said, "Just forget it! Come on, let's go. Judas and his people are on the way to have me arrested. Let's save them some time and meet them halfway."

Just like He said, and I we went over this scene earlier so I'll not go into details with it right now, Judas approaches Jesus and He gets arrested. He gets arrested and Peter is right there and guess what happens?

Yeah. You guessed it! The Bible says, "...once Jesus was arrested **all of the disciples ran and left Him...**" It actually records the event by saying they all "deserted Him and fled."

That makes the 4th time Peter wasn't able to stay by Jesus side no matter what, like he said he would do, and it still wasn't close to morning time!

Finally the story takes us to morning time. Jesus is being interrogated in an outside courtyard by the religious leaders. While they're questioning Him, Peter, who had snuck in amongst the crowd, was approached by a female who accused him of being a friend of Jesus. Peter denied it.

A little while later, someone else approached Peter and said they saw him with Jesus. Peter denied it.

Finally someone else approached him and told Peter his accent gave him away and that he definitely was one of the men with Jesus. This allegation drove Peter over the edge and he started getting mad and basically telling the last accuser to leave him the fuck alone and that there was no way in Hell he was associated with Jesus.

A rooster crowed. A rooster crowed and Peter was ashamed. He was ashamed and humbled and began to cry. The beauty of this event was we learn even though He denied Jesus, he was able to get his shit together later on and write many valuable manuscripts, letters and documents that would be included in the Bible.

When Jesus used the term "truly", it meant what follows was the gospel truth...literally. He told us we are to speak in the language He spoke.

That doesn't mean we have to use "truly" whenever we're trying to make a point. It means we are to keep our answers and statements simple. Here's what He actually said: Let your "yes" be "yes" and your "no" be "no". Simple, right?

There should be no need to step into a courtroom and have to put your hand on a Bible and say, "I swear to God I'm about to tell the truth." Just tell the truth.

There should be no need to tell somebody, "I promise I'm not lying!" Just don't lie.

There are a couple of things I would like you to take away from this book that I want to highlight as sort of a summary. The 1st thing is, if you're studying the Bible and you see Jesus says "truly" and then some other stuff…that other stuff is very important and is going to come true.

The other main thing is to keep it simple. Life is about simplicity. Jesus said you shouldn't be hot or cold when it comes to following Him. If you're warm or in the middle…you're no good to Him or His cause.

The last thing is to learn how to simply say "yes" or "no". You shouldn't have to say "I swear to God" before a statement or "I put that on my mama".

Leave God and your mama out of whatever the fuck you was about to say, keep it simple and just tell the truth.

Alright, I gave you 2 Private Matter Bonus Essays in the body of the book and I'm giving you one more here. It's how strongly I feel about Jesus. Thanks for reading to the end and check this essay out:

JESUS FREAK

There is a term thrown around called "Jesus Freak". It was designed to be a put-down on anybody who was seriously into Jesus. It worked. Well, it worked for a little while. I have to admit, it even worked on me...at first.

Following the Bible and being a Christian has always been a social and religious target for people who want to live life on their own terms. Nobody ever attacks Islam, Buddhism, Darwinism but if you mention you are a Christian or if you mention the name "Jesus", here come the sighs and the "why do you always have to talk about Jesus?" reactions.

Here's why. You know what? I was going to do it in paragraph form, but I just changed my mind. I like list's so I'm going to number some of the reasons why:

1.	Jesus is the only human who ever claimed to know God directly and He had plenty of supporting evidence with His actions.

2.	Jesus is the only human ever whose death was documented and witnessed by many people…and His resurrection was also witnessed and documented by many people.

3.	Jesus is the only human that had documented records where He was able to tell storms to die down and to control nature.

4.	Jesus is the only human who delivered a message that talked about getting personal with the creator of the Universe. All other religious and spiritual paths talk about some "thing" that is not designed for humans to get personal with (Islam being an exception...kind of).

5.	Jesus is the only human who is recorded as performing actual miracles. Miracles that included raising people from the dead.

6.	Jesus is the only human who gave us a clear explanation for human's purpose on Earth AND tied it into our spiritual origins. All other spiritual walks just tell us to do what we think is right and love everybody and we're gonna be A-ok.

7.	Jesus is the only human who has recorded and documented manuscripts written thousands of years before His birth that predicted His coming.

I could go on forever with this list, but I won't. I think

you get the point that Jesus was and is an extraordinary

individual. He spent His adult life here on Earth looking out for

us. His laser-focus was to let us know that God is real, Satan and

sin are real and that since He is the only one who actually

witnessed Earth's beginnings and the rise and fall of Satan and

sin, His goal was to teach us how to duplicate the Kingdom of

Heaven here on Earth.

He also had a ton of lessons about life that, if followed

properly, will make any individual find peace, happiness and

success in every situation in life. He tied right, wrong, good, bad,

God, Heaven, financial and spiritual wealth together in a way

that no one before Him or since Him has been able to do.

If somebody wants to label me as a "Jesus Freak", I gladly

accept that title. Actually, you can call me whatever the fuck

you want to and I won't be offended or mad. In the case of the

"Jesus Freak" label, I will actually shake your hand and thank you. That's a label I will gladly wear.

I have to say something about the "Jesus Freak" thing. A lot of people are finding it fashionable to wear bracelets that say "what would Jesus do" and people like to make social media posts that say "I love Jesus and He is My Lord and Savior. If you agree, please share." And now you got 3,000 mutha fuckas agreeing...but are they actually living like Jesus wants them to?

Do you remember the Lord's prayer? A lot of Believers say that prayer daily or at least a lot. How many of them understand that our purpose on Earth is to create Heaven on Earth? In that prayer, Jesus taught us to ask for "...may your Kingdom come..." That means we are asking for the Kingdom of Heaven to be established on Earth.

How does God work on Earth? Since He gave humans dominion, He rarely just comes in and does whatever He wants to do. He respects His own laws. What God looks for is for humans that He can work through.

The entire Bible if full of recorded events where God has Moses free the slaves, Joshua leading battles and prophets to give messages to world leaders and specific groups of people.

Jesus constantly told people who were interested in His lessons that they had to take action. Believers are supposed to suit up for spiritual warfare. Believers are supposed to stand up against laws that go directly against God's laws such as the legalization of homosexual marriage, corrupt and prejudicial drug sentencing laws and a host of other activity that certain members of society try and legalize so they can try and operate above God's laws.

A real "Jesus Freak" is ready to stand up when the rest of society is bowing down to social pressure. A "Jesus Freak" is an individual who doesn't just wear a *"Jesus" t-shirt* while he or she is actively involved in activities that destroy our temple such as drinking, vaping and letting their bodies get completely out of shape.

I will close with this: "Jesus Freaks" are the true leaders of society. Don't try and wear this badge without putting in the time. Being a "Jesus Freak" is not designed to be a fad. It involves daily prayer, meditation and conversations with our Heavenly Father, with Jesus and with the Holy Spirit.

The key word is "daily". A true "Jesus Freak" does not go to church one hour a week and think that their "God time" quota for the week is satisfied. You don't get to wear the "Jesus Freak" label if that's the only time you tryin' to put in.

"Jesus Freaks", it's time to run shit!!!

It's time to stop being scared to stand up for shit!!!

It's time to stop letting human governments that contradict Heaven's government to continue to fuck shit up!!!

It's time to re-claim your lost shit!!! It's time to start a local Bible Fight Club!!! It's time to do whatever your "Jesus" shirts are telling the world that you do!!!

LET'S DO THIS SHIT FOR REAL, JESUS FREAKS!!!

I'll see the rest of you freaks at the finish line!!!

Personal Development Notes

76